MINNIE WILMARK

TRAVEL CHEAP

The Essential Guide to Traveling on a Budget, Learn Effective Strategies and Useful Tips on How You Can Have Your Dream Getaway on a Budget

Descrierea CIP a Bibliotecii Naţionale a României
MINNIE WILMARK
   TRAVEL CHEAP. The Essential Guide to Traveling on a Budget, Learn Effective Strategies and Useful Tips on How You Can Have Your Dream Getaway on a Budget / Minnie Wilmark – Bucharest: Editura My Ebook, 2020
   ISBN

MINNIE WILMARK

TRAVEL CHEAP

The Essential Guide to Traveling on a Budget, Learn Effective Strategies and Useful Tips on How You Can Have Your Dream Getaway on a Budget

My Ebook Publishing House
Bucharest, 2020

TRAVEL CHEAP

The Essential Guide to Traveling on a Budget, Learn Effective Strategies and Useful Tips on How You Can Have Your Dream Getaway on a Budget

My Book Publishing House
Budapest, 2021

TABLE OF CONTENTS

- ground-transportation and other means of transportation while on the trip
- Accommodation, Meals and special events

Travel dynamics and process

- Before getting there - Planning for the trip
- Getting there
- Arriving and while at destination – maximizing your trip and stay
- The trip back – getting back home safely and cheaply

Travel wrap-up

- Post-assessment and budgeting

General tips

- 101 tips for traveling on a budget

Addendum

- Checklists and Other Money-related matters when traveling

THE TRAVEL PHENOMENON

INTRODUCTION

The key to budget travel is to plan ahead. When it comes to *family trips, globetrotting, well-deserved vacations* and/or *going to see new places we have never been before, the reality of cost and budgeting is always in the back of our minds.*

Planning and spending our travel dollar wisely is a priority for most families. Curbing spending and costs, while still enjoying your vacation to its fullest, is the key to guaranteed success and fiscal responsibility. *Your pocketbook and family will thank you!*

The reasoning behind saving money while traveling is simple: Even if your personal budget is extremely tight, you can still take a break and enjoy life! *Simply put*, life is just too short to never step out of the door or leaving the homestead!

Also remembering that while traveling, whether on a budget or not, **even the smallest of things can all add op to a large vacation or travel bill!**

For example, all those hotel extra's, cab-fares, tips, restaurants, car rentals, gas for your own vehicle if on a road trip, tickets for special attractions or events, beach-and-pool-side drinks (if not at an all- inclusive resort or cruise) and more, adds on and piles up!

This brings us to the some of the rhyme and reason behind budgeting for travel and planning well. This also applies monetarily, to ensure your trip is a success, enjoyable and memorable. Your outlook could be a balance between replenishing your resources and *not breaking the bank in the process*!

'101 Tips for Traveling on a budget' is a quick-guide meant to assist you with this task. Its handy, easy-reference format provides you with topical information regarding all aspects of your planned trip. Find relevant tips in these pages meant to assist you in any travel undertaking in the near or foreseeable future. *It is all about saving you money on your travel endeavors.*

When choosing to travel, most of us are normally doing so *with our families,* opting for *destination travel* and taking that *well-deserved vacation of a lifetime* or all of the above.

This guide will offer tips and insights on how to customize, optimize, maximize and personalize your travel experience every step of the way. Through this process, travelers attend pro-actively to the impact of decisions.

There are many un-seized opportunities to save some cash in the process. We will briefly uncover less known and obvious financial detail, affordability, aftermath and fiscal strategy as it pertains to travel locally, domestically or abroad.

Here's to finding some savings and cash tips as you explore these pages and the world!

Maybe you are in the early phases of planning or booking your trip, shopping around online or checking some websites or travel magazines. Some of us might even be thinking of calling some travel agents to do our homework upfront.

Perhaps you have not taken a trip in a very long time and find yourself in desperate need of a good breakaway vacation to remember. Maybe you are a young student backpacking and exploring some corners of this wonderful world we live in, or a retired couple enjoying the travel scene together.

Whatever your situation and reason for travel, we trust you will potentially find something in these pages that will inspire you and save you some money in the process.

To get us started, here is the first tip for all the procrastinators, impulse travel buyers, discount bargain hunters and vacation shoppers amongst us.

"The reason most people never reach their goals is that they don't define them, learn about them, or ever seriously consider them as believable or achievable." Denis Waitley

---

TIP # 1: Make a list of some; any or all of the destinations you would like to visit in your lifetime... and then plan to get to at least one this year!

Like anything else in life, travel needs to be planned for somewhat. It is almost like setting a short- time 'SMART' goal for leisure and vacationing. Marketers of time-share and destination vacations, often refer to this as an argument to invest in a travel solution.

People often suggest that we treat travel or vacationing, like any other planned financial decision in life. This is all irrespective of whether this includes house, car, tuition, health, insurance or other life-expense. Travel and vacation is justified and 'sold', as just another important item on the list to think about and budget for.

Setting goals is described and accepted as a powerful tool to achieve success and keeps people motivated.

Out of the list of **dream destinations** you just made or have in mind, you cannot possibly achieve reaching all of them, and nor should you perhaps. One can but wish and dream ... Going after these dreams in a planned fashion, will mean a significant investment of time, money, energy, talent, and opportunities. *You will need to prioritize.*

Prioritizing should include travel items, trips, goals and destinations that you really desire to visit, see, conquer, treasure, explore and would love to achieve in your lifetime.

Realizing of course that these 'dreams' though, might not all be achievable immediately, or at all. You need to view this as a wish list, shortlist eventually becoming checklist! Then, move on to making at least the first goal or location visit on the list happen this year! (Alternatively, as soon as funds allow and you are able to make it happen).

Hands-on work, defining and planning for travel in such a way that it will convey an actual goal or goals, destinations, budgets and periods.

A goal, in order to be effective and drive people towards it, should have the following characteristics. The goal should be Specific, Measurable, Action-oriented, Realistic, and Time- constrained. In other words, it must be a SMART goal, (as referred to earlier).

SPECIFIC: The travel goal(s) should be specific. Detail is what matters here. Avoid generalizations; get to the point and crux of the matter. Specify your immediate travel needs and means. Then plan to go after it pro-actively.

For example, take that tropical island, destination dream vacation: "I have always wanted to ..." seems a little general when compared to **'I will travel, with my family to Hawaii for a vacation of two weeks within the next six months.'**

MEASURABLE: The SMART travel goal must be measurable. This goes along with being specific. A goal defined specifically might already be measurable. The abovementioned goal stated intention, involved parties, location, purpose and a timeframe – all measurable elements.

A measurable travel goal, like going to Hawaii, with a family of four, including two children under the age of five, within the next six months helps you identify, plan, execute and track more efficiently and increase your odds of actually making it there! Considering the logistics in this fashion, makes it that more realistic to enable your family to take the planned trip of a lifetime, as opposed to just dreaming about it!

ACTION-ORIENTED: A SMART goal must also be action oriented. It cannot merely be stated. You must relate the goal to doing something, to indicate what needs to be done. An action verb will indicate what needs to be accomplished. "I will travel" is a good example of an action statement, stated intent and implies preparation and planning, will and persistence.

REALISTIC: For any goal to be motivational and get you committed to reaching it, it must be realistic. When a goal is not realistic and the person does not really believe it can be reached, then the commitment is lacking and the effort will not be there to permit the goal to be realized.

Choosing realistic goals are based on your present status. What jumps to mind right away in our example, is whether and how you can afford it and make it happen! (Hopefully this guide can also offer some tips to get your there).

TIME-CONSTRAINED: In order for a goal to move people towards it, it must be time-constrained. A timeline needs to be associated with it. It will entice people to move towards the goal. The timeline set, will be based on the goal itself and the present status. Six months is stated here as a realistic timeline, leaving enough time to save for, plan, book and take your well-deserved vacation to Hawaii (as in our stated example),OR anywhere else YOU have chosen to go!

With these SMART goal insights in mind, the *101 TIPS* are divided into four perspectives if you will, for an easy reference-framework. These 'categories' almost are marked by the following keywords, sometimes stated explicitly, sometimes implied and self-explanatory, inferred and or assumed. They will appeal to the money-conscious and budget-savvy would-be and seasoned travelers alike.

▪ **SAVE MONEY**, shares suggestions on hotels, car rentals, airfare, destination travel, food, maximize discounts, comparison-shop, special offers, insider-tips and more to put more hard cash in your travel pocket.

- **AVOID COST** and costly mistakes, deals with impulse buying, un-reputable travel service providers, traveling without insurance, always read the fine print, buyer beware and other insights that will help you hold onto your travel dollar or spend it appropriately on what you want.

- **ENSURE DETAILS**, involves paying close attention to confirming details, fine-print, insurance and other travel-related issues

- **BE SMART**, will be offering travelers, general travel tips, as not only formulated in SMART goals, but also translating well into being an informed consumer, making wise choices and decisions on all their travel endeavors. Our acronym below summarizes the advantages and of budget-driven, planned travel for your inference and reflection:

S - Smart, well informed and structured

m – Memorable, miles

a - advantage

r - Rigorous and regular

t - Thorough

In short, "101 Tips on traveling on a budget" strives to be a travel companion and tool. The intention with this guide is to assist and enable world explorers and bag-toting travelers everywhere, to becoming frugal, informed, happy, innovative, creative, spend-thrift-averse and prepared travelers. Even when traveling on a limited or shoestring budget!

TRAVEL-ENABLERS

Financial Strategies and Budgeting for a vacation or trip

Most people mistakenly think that you need a lot of money to travel, or that vacations are simply too expensive and lavish. This is a good example of a wrongful assumption. Traveling 'light' so to speak, with limited cash, combined with a positive attitude and a deep personal commitment, persistence and resourcefulness is possible.

Simply put, *planning pays* and *travel budgets save money*. Taking the extra time to review sources at your disposal prior to, during and after your trip encourages a hands-on, pro-active approach to traveling and vacationing in general.

Most of us want to focus on having a good time and ensuring that a couple of the smaller details are taken care of. Taking advantage of saving opportunities and discounts, limited offers and utilizing tips and tricks from frequent travelers seem to be the keys to travel success.

Lessons learned will serve us all well when taking our next trip, whether to the campgrounds, some exotic tropical paradise or both!

There are various useful information and travel sources to assist you in this money-saving undertaking for traveling on a budget:

- web-pages and online providers who specialize in hot deals for vacation package bargains,

- travel websites brokerages and discount fare operators, airline carriers and websites with last minute fares and seat sales,

- travel specialist portals like priceline.com where taking advantage of overnight flight flights, empty seats and multiple connections and other ways to save money while traveling the globe, is a mastered art of comparison-shopping and the budget travelers paradise so to speak.

- Printed material, budget travel magazines (like Arthur Frommer's Budget Travel Magazine and Bestfares

- Other specific budget-travel, industry-related publications and resources like: "First-Time: Around the World," by Doug Lansky (published by "Rough Guides") or "The Travel Detective: How to Get the Best Service and the Best Deals from Airlines, Hotels, Cruise Ships, and Car Rental Agencies," by Peter Greenberg (Random House) or the ever-handy: "The Traveler's Handbook," published by Globe Pequot Press.

- Various customized, targeted guidebooks like, "Let's Go," guidebooks by and for students, are ideal for backpacking and exploring Europe for example. "Lonely Planet," guidebooks to remote and or popular destinations of choice, with lots of valuable information for both upscale and budget travelers

- Travel Word-of-mouth from regular travelers, colleagues, family and friends who travel frequently often share great insights. We cannot discount these value-adding insights.

- Coupons and special vouchers, Family discounts and specials, online, limited-time internet- bargains

- Condominium or developers, resort, time-share Promotions. Sales-pitch pop-up windows, Camping (sites and cabins, bring own linens and towels), tourist boards and information centers, and many more...

Setting up a quick quote or cost-analysis for your planned journey, a rough travel expense account or budgeting outline to get started, is always a good idea to give your dreams some wings.

At the very least, you will have an idea and some kind of baseline and starting point. Initially though, forget all about expensive restaurants, business class flights and luxury car rentals and all you might have to sacrifice or cannot have on your budget, at least for now.

All you need to know, upfront, is that **YOU *CAN* TRAVEL IN STYLE ON A BUDGET** and *101 Tips for Traveling on a budget* **will offer a few ideas to keep the** money where it should be – in your pocket and/or well spent to make your vacation dream come true, while still maximizing your vacationing and travel experience!

THE TRAVEL DILEMMA AND DECISION

Where and when to go, where to stay, how to get there Destination Travel

Traveling is both exciting and exhilarating. It appeals to the majority of us for various reasons. It all seems to stem from somewhere deep within our human make-up. We are social and curious beings. Our earlier nomadic traditions and heritage, urge us to explore and conquer our world, both known and unknown. It has always been a quest and inspiration to go somewhere we have not been before and see places unseen until now.

The travel dilemma most of us face is simply when and where to take our next trip or vacation for leisure purposes. We will look briefly at a couple of money-saving tips that will help us answer a couple of key questions: How do I pick a travel destination and when can/is it best to take my annual vacation?

or Can I fit in a couple of short trips this year and where would I go?

Actually making the decision about where to go and when to travel is the easy part. It does not matter if we are traveling as sun or adventure seekers, to see family or people we know at a certain location or country, attend a spectacular or special event, visiting an exotic destination or just simply looking for peace and quiet.

The best time to start planning your trip is when the impulse hits you! Send away for information right away. Contact the local state and National tourist offices and check online, to learn more about your destination of choice.

Plan your trip so everyone has fun and budget for it accordingly! Think child-centered activities or a personal interest indulgence. Save money by deciding early and balance the family interest. Avoid trying to fit in all the "touristy" must-sees that will add up in the end. Select a few of them you really cannot bear to miss and enjoy them together.

Ensure the details are taken care of, like how early or late the attraction is open, transportation to and from the location and be smart by wearing flat shoes and taking water along for in case the wait is longer than expected. Remember, everyone else will be eager to see what he or she came to see too. It might take a little longer at popular venues, so plan your itinerary accordingly.

Deciding the duration of your trip, how long and how you will travel, are all-important considerations. The sooner and earlier you plan and budget, the better prepared and more informed you would be. "The early bird catches the worm", we always say, and, "First come, First serve".

You can save a lot of money by booking early and taking advantages of special offers, seat sales and more. Scout for good deals. Watch out and avoid deals that sound too good to be true (they normally are!). Do not get caught by ill-reputed providers and travel-scams. Always read the fine print!

Beware of other details like, what time of year you choose to travel, what the weather will be like, the impact of seasonal traveling, public or special holidays and more. Be smart and budget for the unexpected, delays, unplanned extended stays, inevitable layovers and more. Show some resilience, positive attitude and utilize your financial resourcefulness to make the most of your trips, regardless of what life and fate throws at you!

Early on, while in planning and information gathering mode, consulting with a travel agent, professional specialist, tap into their expertise and experience. They can easily provide

24

current information, industry updates, possibilities and pricing, availability, plan and book vacations; find you big discounts and special deals.

They will also be able to point out details that would otherwise remain hidden and unconsidered like new resorts, airport construction updates and hang-ups. Some can be extremely resourceful, patient and imaginative and want to provide you with the best travel and customer service options and solutions that are right for you.

They mostly work on a commission basis though, so just ensure that this is the best deal for YOU and not their pocketbook alone! Save money by asking many questions and pose the question about discounts. If you do not ask, they will not necessarily offer the cheapest option or hunt for better deals!

When deciding to travel as a single individual or a couple, double rooms in a hotel are mostly cheaper than a single room. Consider sharing, but choose and weigh your travel partner(s) wisely!

Ensure that you are financially independent of one another and that all parties are responsible with money and will not come running to you expecting to help. Clarify needs and wants and highlight some mutual respect for these.

Ask the question of whether personal habits are compatible. How would they react in crisis-mode? These factors are handy to know in advance, in order to prepare you for anything. Save money by protecting your financial interests. Avoid others taking advantage of you, and you, ending up paying for mostly everything and sponsoring extravagant spenders. The onus is on you to ensure you take care of every detail.

This would include who and how you will pay for what. Discuss and stipulate it literally to ensure all parties are informed. Then clarify and agree on it. Be smart and act early to sort out any differences and avoid conflict and disagreement. Schedule regular time apart and pool some of your money into a 'kitty' to pay for outings and entertainment.

Guidebook-like informational tools should not dictate your trip. They describe, should not prescribe! Some might have set itineraries and must sees that do not interest you necessarily and might be costly if you choose to follow it to a tee. Their pricing options might also be out-of-date, so check their accuracy. They are good and useful for pricing options and ranges that again are useful in the travel budgeting process and list numerous lodging options across the spectrum. This highlights choice and empowered decision making.

Another consideration is Ecotourism. Consider carriers and travel providers that advocate and practice sustainable, safer and environmentally friendly options for travel. It has less impact on the environment and does not disrupt the local economy. On the contrary, it utilizes supports and optimizes it!

It is all still about making the most of your trip and seeing any and all that you want to, experience and enjoy your travel and quest. Stroll, walk, take it easy on your first day and do not try to fit everything into 24 hours! In short: Go somewhere! Go anywhere! BUT DO GO!

Travel logistics: trips, bookings and travel details
Destination, location, type and duration of trip
Means of getting to and from, airfare
Ground-transportation while on the trip
Accommodation, Meals and special events

When considering a trip or planning any kind of travel, it is important to plan for the unexpected and consider the financial side of things early on. This ensures affordability, liquidity and having the resources to enjoy it to the fullest!

101 Tips for traveling on a budget focuses on this aspect in more detail.

When budgeting, plan for the worst-case scenario money wise. Prepare for things to cost a little more than you expected. Keep and eye on the exchange rate (if applicable). Allow up to 20% increase in cost to be on the safe side of things.

It is extremely easy these days to have access to your financial resources through ATM's and credit cards. Just remember that it is just as easy to overspend because of it being so readily available. A little discipline will go a long way to protect your financial interest and help you stick to your travel budget.

Set some spending priorities and criteria in advance, like eating well, even if this means sacrificing a bit on lodgings or visa versa, depending on what is more important to you. Think about value and cost in the local currency as opposed to converting all the time to your home-currency and comparing and weighing prices that way.

Carrying some spare cash somewhere can be a lifesaver. The rule of thumb seems to be around $50-$100 US equivalent, in small bills. This can be used for incidentals, ground-transportation like cab fare and/or your return home, tips and more.

When considering when, where, how, for how long and what type of vacation, trip or holiday venture to undertake, we all get caught up in the anticipation, excitement and exhilaration.

Sometimes we let the more important financial side of things slip a little. After all, for most of us, this only happens a couple of times in our lifetime or perhaps once a year. We tend to indulge and forget about our pocket book a little. However, some close attention to the financials now and during your trip, will save you lots of headaches and interest charges on your credit card balances later! You will thank yourself for your fiscal restraint and spending discipline, upfront planning, foresight and forward thinking!

There are many ways to save money, avoid unnecessary cost, ensure you take care of details end up a smart and perceptive traveler. We look at a couple of suggestions in this section offering some handy tips in handling the logistics of your trip, in effect optimizing traveling on a budget and making your travel dollar go further!

Road trips - saving money while traveling by car

- **Maximize gas mileage and efficiency.** A well-maintained vehicle will go a long way to ensure carefree driving. It is advisable to travel in a small economy car. It could be your own or a rental. However, bear in mind, the smaller the vehicle, and the better it will be on gas. Minivans and sport utility vehicles are practical only if you have to transport a large family and lots of equipment or luggage.

- **Keeping yourself and others entertained while on the road is no small task**. Music or books on tape or CD, signed out from your local library, can be a lifesaver. Solo driving can become extremely boring especially when all others have nodded off and all falls silent.

However, when you are actively listening, on the edge of your driver's seat so to speak while listening to a novel or mystery, the time passes by quite quickly.

- **Pack-a-snack.** Bring your own refreshments and snacks. Gas station prices on drinks and snack food are high. Avoid these during a pit stop, if you are counting your travel dollars. A cooler packed with lots of cool drinks, water and ice and/or a thermos of coffee or hot water for tea, some fruit, granola bars, or a sandwich, goes a long way to still the hunger and save you money by avoiding all high priced stops en route.

- **Gas fill-ups.** For filling up your car en route, avoid pushing to the limit until the gas runs out or filling up at or in remote locations. The rationale in this statement: gas will obviously be more expensive, the more remote or isolated the station is. If you miscalculated and the light on the dashboard indicates that you are really in need, opt for filling just half a tank until you reach the next more densely or major populated destination, where gas might be a little cheaper.

- **Travel necessities.** It is advisable to be traveling with basic value-add necessities, like a cell phone and a first aid kit. Both can prove to be essential in emergencies.

- **Communication needs.** A handy short-term cell phone rental might be the answer for and on your trip. The peace of mind it offers, might just be worth the price, trouble and investment. Cell phone long distance calls are still cheaper than ones made from hotels or resorts. They typically add some hefty surcharges and tend to charge higher long distance rates.

Traveling Baggage

Next, our discussion turns to luggage. What exactly do you need to pack into your suitcase and how? What goes into your suitcase is important too.

- Shop for the items you need several days before your trip to avoid last minute convenience buying

- Empty cheap dollar-store equivalent plastic bottles filled with products like shampoo and liquid soap will go a long way to save you some money. Buyers beware of travel size items. Typically, you do not find these items economically priced. Mostly people can consider them a luxury and specialized item. Soap dish and toothbrush cases are also handy items to store your wet bathroom utilities in and keep your clothes dry.

- Invest in a customized and general mini drugstore with various basic items like aspirin, band- aids, antacids, and cold remedies When in need the hotel convenient store or local pharmacy prices can be astronomically and notoriously over-priced.

- Back-to-the-basics: always have an extra pair of socks, pantyhose, and underwear somewhere. Be prepared for anything and everything, including delays. If there are delays on your return trip, for any reason, it is reassuring to know that you will at least have fresh undergarments to wear!

- Pack wisely and include a couple of extra outfits. Hotel dry-cleaning is expensive and having a quick change of clothes for a spill or other inevitabilities is always a good idea. Pack more than you need seems to be the rule of thumb.

- Liquid laundry soap can be a good investment for clothing that needs a little spot cleaning or laundering, hand washing it in the sink will also save you a dollar or two while en route.

- A trusted toiletry bag, stocked with all you might need, ready to go is always a good idea.

Having your toiletry and bathroom essentials ready at all, times will reduce the likelihood of forgetting something important like your toothbrush and having to buy one.

Hotels – hotel coupons or room savers (online)

- Check with the hotel if they have a frequent guest plan

- Ask about package deals

- If attending a conference, ask for the delegate rate

- Explore other options than hotels - homes, apartments, guest rooms and houses, B&B's , sub-let or short-term 'lease'-like agreements for example: rent a Florida house for a month, staying with family or friends, relatives or business contacts, farmhouses, self-catering apartments, Monasteries and convents in Europe are also cheaper options

- Avoid big Hotel bills, try AAA memberships, family-friendly hotels, ask for a first floor room, as most have pools (if you are fearful for little children wandering around and falling in).

- continental breakfasts are a great money-saver for large families

- Ask about any reduced fares at hotels, consider last-minute check-ins – hotels are rarely really fully booked

- Eating in a supermarket deli-like counter proves to be much cheaper than fast-food locations or expensive restaurants

In The Air

- Explore offerings online, comparison shop and booking with discount airlines are all smart strategies. Remember flexibility on your part regarding dates and times will translate into savings.

- Enroll in an air miles, reward or frequent flyer plan that often includes discounts on hotels and car rentals.

- Timing is everything. Avoid peak periods for example, holidays, spring break, and peak business hour time's makes for more travelers en route and supply and demand will dictate pricing and cost – usually higher.

Take advantage of shoulder and low season travel periods.

- Best airfare rates often involve a Saturday night stay.

- Book flights at least two weeks in advance. The closer the booking to the flight date, the more expensive it will be.

- Log on to the airline's website and check out unadvertised flight specials.

- Booking on-line usually saves a few dollars too.

- Use a park-and-fly service and park your own vehicle at the airport. Driving your car there and back is much cheaper than a taxi if you live far from the airport. There are also airport bus services or shuttles that are cheaper than taxis.

- When boarding the plane, bring your own water. Airplanes are dry and flight attendants do not have time to keep refilling your glass.

- Never eat at the airport. Airport food is twice the price of food anywhere else. Try to eat before arriving at the airport or pack a few snacks to tie you over until you reach your destination.

- Once on the ground, ask the information desk about free shuttles to your hotel or use public transit.

- Save time and headaches by traveling with a bag, you can carry on the plane. Some airlines have express check-in counters for passengers traveling with carry-on luggage only.

Transportation

- Travel passes for public or mass transportation offers a good deal and can save you some money.

- Shuttles or trains are often cheaper than flights, sharing cab-fares if traveling alone

- Taxis are convenient but rarely worth the price. If you do hire a taxi, consider asking someone to split the fare with you.

These savings suggestions, are listed here as introductory comments and serve as teasers to lead into some of the more details 101 Tips that follow nearer to the end of this booklet. Stay tuned as we move onto the next section.

Travel dynamics and process

Before getting there - Planning for the trip

Getting there

Arriving and while at destination, maximizing your trip and stay

The trip back – getting back home safely and cheaply

Whether making plans early to ensure availability and locking in a price, or flexible enough to wait until last minute and or deeply discounted fares and travel deals, there are options to suit every pocket, taste and travel budget!

Investing in trip cancellation insurance and travel medical insurance are travel necessities you cannot dismiss, discard or under-estimate. This is not the spot to be thinking cost cutting. Protect your travel investment best you can.

If traveling on an international flight, re-confirm your booking 72 hours prior to departure – some charter companies reserve the right to cancel your booking if you do not! When confirmed on a domestic flight, airlines cannot bump you. Try to get plenty of sleep the night before your trip. Call to find out whether there are any delays before leaving for the airport.

Having an 'out-the-door checklist' prior to departure and before returning home, with a few miscellaneous items to pack, as a last minute reminder, always proves helpful and avoids unnecessary stressful moments and wasteful and hasty cash purchases. It might contain any, some or all of the following:

- First aid kits should contain, at the very least some band-aids and anti-bacterial ointment, all prescriptions, cold and allergy medicines, dosage spoon and chart. Tylenol for the traveling adults, children and babies is always a good idea as well.

- Foil-packaged, coffee and tea are a necessity. You can also pack, if you prefer a certain type, Sweeteners and Cream/Milk or whitener.

- Camera and film supplies

- All relevant travel documents, tickets, passports, birth certificates, travel insurance information, baggage, currency and travelers checks (if applicable), Phone numbers and maps, emergency contact and identification cards for the kids and individual travelers

- Addresses for sending postcards, and stamps, Cell phone and/or prepaid phone card

- Favorite books, music, DVD's and videos for the children (most hotels have VCRs now)

- Bathing suits, extra towels, and sunscreen

- Snacks and juice or water for the hotel (every penny counts)

- Finally yet importantly… do not forget the EXTRA pillows and favorite toy or sleeping friend for the kid(s) if required or deemed a necessity!

Ensure to set and arrange for a couple of alarm clocks or wake-up calls on your day of departure. Confirm ground transportation to and from the airport if you are not driving yourself and using the park-and-fly service. Allow lots of transit and en route times. Confirm your bookings and remember to always let hotels or resorts know if you are running late, delayed and or if your trip is cancelled altogether.

Utilize travel services, that is why they are there, remembering that all extras like valet parking, baggage handling, luggage carts, tips etc. all add up and need to be budgetary items or categories in your overall travel and financial plan.

For the budget conscious, select the neighborhood-friendly hotel that caters to the local crowd, not the pricy touristy options. You might be surprised at the value and hospitality you might find. Make the concierge your friend and information centre – they are the main link to the corner of the world you find yourself in. Get that special insider and local insights, tips and expertise at your disposal, waiting to make your trip and experience that more special and memorable.

They can also offer some handy referrals and give ideas on what things might cost, book ground transportation and much, much more.

There are always also hostels, YMCA, and YWCA's that are clean, safe and reliable. If visiting multiple cities, picking one hotel chain might also be more convenient and save you time and money in the process.

A discussion on travel logistics, dynamics and process would not be complete, without mentioning safety and security. A couple of tips follow:

- Do not travel with precious possessions and be discreet with cash and other valuables. Leave sentimental and irreplaceable items at home preferably.

- Protect your essentials like travel documentation, passport, traveler's checks, credit cards and more. Concealing them on-person, in a pouch or somewhere in your clothing is all accepted practice.

- Be watchful but not paranoid about being at risk of becoming or being a robbery victim. You will end up spending excessive money on cabs everywhere as opposed to taking a gentle stroll and or exploring by foot!

- Keep valuables concealed in crowded places. Do not consider hip pockets and dangling bags good places for your wallet!

- Do not carry excess cash you do not need, especially at night and do not flaunt cash in public under any circumstance. Do not make yourself a visible and easy target.

- Divide and spread your cash and other money instruments like traveler's checks around your luggage – do not carry it all in one place.

- A good budgeting tip is wrapping your wallet with a rubber band or two to make it harder for pickpockets to remove it from your pocket without detection!

- Keep your luggage safe, with you and secure at night when you sleep.

- Never leave luggage and or valuables in a car, bus, taxi, train or other form of transportation.

- Always watch at security screenings and customs checks to ensure that your belongings do not disappear.

- Speaking about customs, when exceeding the duty-free limits, know that it will cost you dearly, up to as much as 10 % on the next $1000 worth of goods.

- If you purchased many items (over $50 each) and mailed them to yourself, they are still dutiable. Personal items can be shipped home and you will not have to pay duties if returning them to your destination as long as you write on the package "American goods returned" for example.

This might not be the case for other locations, so verify this with your mail carrier beforehand. Again, planning well ensures an informed consumer. These steps can and will save you money, avoid costly errors and or oversights. Attention to detail will assist you in being a smart, well- informed, money-conscious and dollar-and-cents saving traveler.

Again, most of these statement and suggestions are general in terms and do not necessarily list every time how you will be able to save money, avoid cost, benefit from paying attention to detail and be a savvy, money-saving and SMART traveler. It will mostly do so through implied inference and deduction, you will be able to come up with your own interpretation of how these tips can help you save money.

That is the bonus of budgeting, planning and the format of this tips-guide. You can take as little or as much as you need, relevant to your trip and customize and tailor it into a strategy that is right and suitable, appropriate and guarantees savings for your unique circumstance, means and action travel plans and budgets.

Travel wrap-up

Post-assessment and budgeting

100 General tips for traveling on a budget

This brings up the final point in our discussion, before getting to the 100 numbered tips that are left for you to scrutinize and explore.

Once you get home, with all your receipts, bills, photographs (or film, memory cards these days!) in one piece and your dream vacation has come to an end, spend a couple of minutes on a debrief or post-mortem so to speak.

If you are jetlagged and just simply have no energy to do so, wait a couple of days. However, do not delay or postpone for too long, because we are creatures of habit and fall right back into life, without sparing a second thought of our trips' aftermath and how lessons learnt, money saved and more, can assist us on our next round of travel.

This situation-analysis and post-assessment will be helpful in that the budget-plan now almost takes care of itself and will just need to be adjusted and a new destination , facts and amounts filled in to set you up nicely for the checking off that next dream location or trip you had in mind and listed earlier.

In addition to all the money-saving tips embedded, highlighted and given so far, we took the liberty of assembling from various trusted travel sources, both in print and online, *101 tips for traveling on a budget*, listed here for your quick reference and use. There might not always be a specific financial benefit or key learning in everyone of them, but the underlying logic and stated fact or examples will be self-explanatory.

The added benefit of listing the 100 general tips for traveling on a budget in this manner is that you just choose the ones you need to remember. If all 100 apply and you get value from them, that is great. Choosing a couple specifically because they will have maximum impact for you and enable your trip sooner is even better. Hand selecting the ones you know will stretch your travel dollars and give you the trip of a lifetime our highest goal.

Have FUN with the 100 tips! Customize and personalize them, combine, analyze, synergize and review them. Optimize and utilize them to your heart's content, Add your own, keep the list growing and share these, other and your individual insights with others, inspiring them to undertake and join the global quest and go somewhere, anywhere, or just plan and budget, then GO!

Hope you find something to make your travel dollar stretch a little further and bring that dream vacation one-step closer!

"A journey is a person in itself--no two are alike." **John Steinbeck,** *Travels with Charley*

Tip # 1 through 101

Getting to make the most of your next personal journey.
Remember: "the devil is always in the details".
There are many ways you can <u>save money</u>, <u>avoid costs</u>, <u>ensure details and relevant issues are taken into consideration and dealt with accordingly.</u>

Finding ways to be smart, becoming and being a perceptive traveler, maximizing your travel dollar is as easy as 1, 2,3...(or more accurately, 100!!). Make your pick!

Bearing in mind that we have already covered tip # 1, which dealt with setting SMART travel goals, we now continue with our in-depth list of 101 tips for traveling on a budget.

2. **Arm yourself with lots of information regarding your destination of choice.** Write to obtain information from a variety of sources like the tourism boards, local chamber of commerce and tourist information centers.

They all offer and share information gladly with would-be travelers. Best of all, it costs you only the time and maybe the phone call or postage required on a self-addressed stamped envelope, to access this treasure-trove of information.

Sometimes the information is even online, at your fingertips, readily accessible and without any associated costs. Knowledge is power! It will **save** you money.

Avoid being taken advantage of, exploited or extorted by excessive prices and/or misrepresentation by arming yourself with the facts!

Ensuring that you are familiar with as much background and localized, relevant, up-to-date travel, general information, will better prepare you for the details of your trip, assist in planning your event schedule more effectively, and **being a** smart and informed tourist never hurt anyone! On the contrary, you will maximize your trip, from departure, during to your safe return.

3. **Travel resources and destination guides are a great help and good place to start gathering topical, destination and relevant information.** Consult many of them and check often for new and helpful resources in print and online that contains destination-like travel information.

Save money if you are an AAA member and take advantage of their free travel guides. **Avoid** costly mistakes and unanticipated costs, for hotels for example, by knowing what is happening in the area at the time you are planning to take your trip.

Are there any conventions, major sports events or concerts, tradeshows and other happenings in and around where you plan to be? Might any of these factors influence cost and availability? **Ensure informational detail** provided is reliable and current. **Be smart**, check, and verify the information provided to ensure that it is up to date and accurate.

4. **Be informed and show local interest. Read and do research about your destination, location and surrounding areas.** Hidden treasures are found this way! Enjoy travel

previews and other multi-media sources that can be a good way to "rehearse" and prepare for your trip. Talk to others who have been there and ask them about places to stay and things to see.

5. **Remember to budget some additional funds for taking care of those dear ones who cannot do so for themselves. We are referring to our animal friends and pets.** Special arrangements for pets should be made prior to any trip and well in advance. This applies, whether pets are being cared for at home by a neighbor or friend, placed in a kennel (taking a mini-vacation of their own!), or accompanying you on your trip.

Save money by checking your options at your destination. Some rental vacation homes, apartments, hotels and resorts are pet-friendly and encourage owners to bring them along. **Avoid** unnecessary costs of boarding. Make it a rule of thumb however, to verify any **details** pertaining to animals, prior to departure. **Be smart** and get all vet visits, guidelines, travel documents and other paperwork that applies, done way in advance. If you do not have any pets, looking after your domicile and belongings should be left to a trusted and responsible party you trust and value.

6. **Being practical goes a long way to save you money and unnecessary, self-inflicted 'pain' away from home!** Be sure to pack some common sense too. Save money by not giving in to impulse shopping repeatedly, especially on 'must-have' shoes! Avoid wearing or trying out the newly bought pair of semi-uncomfortable shoes on your travels. Your feet and pocketbook will thank you.

7. **In preparation for making your travel dream come true, assembling a personal travel file is also not a bad idea.** Include the exotic and far-away lands you are considering, as well as your local visitor's attractions and destinations in and around where you live, for those shorter trips. This will assist you in realizing your travel goals and dreams you worked so hard on putting together and getting ready to execute!

8. **Travel documents should always be kept safe and taking a photocopy packed somewhere** is prudent and smart. It will help you to prove your citizenship anywhere, anytime, protecting your personal interest. If it should ever be stolen, contact and share that information with the authorities, embassy and police right away.

9. **There are many options for the health and price-conscious traveler amongst us.** Biking and walking tours are unique options for the adventurous and active types looking for something a little different and or off the beaten path. A good investment in your health, fitness and wellbeing as well as exploring corners of the planet you have not seen or considered before might appeal to you too.

10. **Checking on all travel document requirements for various areas and countries as well as special documentation requirements, entry fees, duties and taxes,** need to be considered, planned and budgeted for. Contacting embassies and getting information on visas and any and all other applicable fees are crucial to minimize the impact on your pocketbook.

11. In a time when technology is so part of our lives, we barely give it a second thought. **It is however very wise to have handy proof of purchase or receipts for any high-tech equipment you might be transporting.** Shortlist your inventory of cameras, radios, camcorders, laptop computers, etc., you are taking with and keep them all in a file.

This could be your redeeming feature when clearing customs and them wanting to charge you duty on these. It is useful to have to ensure minimum delay and no additional cost. Do this even if the items were purchased before traveling. Spending the time on this now way in advance of your planned trip, will ensure smooth sailing and saved dollar down the road. It is definitely worth the effort. Holding on to receipts for newly purchased items, also assists you upon your return to consolidate spending and assess cost, as you wrap up your vacation expenditures, budget and plan for the next trip!

12. **Having the ability of mobility when you are traveling away from home is very important.** Driving yourself around gives you more options to customize and optimize your sightseeing and trip to your liking and individual preference. An enabler of this is your driver license. For most of us, our current license to operate a vehicle should be valid in most of Europe and around the world, for a limited time. HOWEVER, never assume! Always check the details as some countries will still require an international license or permit. Check with your local Department of Motor Vehicles for additional information.

13. **Financial and currency exchange information.** Always be informed, prudent and curious about foreign currency

exchange, rates and related subjects that could affect your travel dollar and cash on hand.

There are numerous sources of this information handy to travelers. You can find out any of the current exchange rates in real-time, from the worldwide Web, stock exchange websites, your own bank, and or by contacting private currency exchange businesses like Thomas Cook and others, offering this financial service.

14. **Taking care of feeding and fueling the human machine is important**. When traveling, it is all about energy and stamina. How far can you go and keep on going? Whether on a led tour or even for traveling alone, it is wise to have handy some 'snack packs' and tit-bits.

These could include raisins, nuts, cheese and crackers, small foil envelopes of tea and coffee, and fresh fruit. Instant breakfast drinks might also help to replenish and re-energize, when you need it most. Having a snack handy or as a quick pick-me-up, could be a lifesaver and is considered a necessity, not a luxury! It will also save you money and exercising the option to have "healthy" alternatives on-hand, will keep you protected from that dreaded holiday pounds that add on so quickly as well!

15. **Verify flight details down to the smallest detail**. Ensure you can answer questions about your trip and are knowledgeable about the terminology used on your booking and ticket. For example: What is the difference between non-stop and direct flights? Yes, the price mostly!

BUT ALSO: Non-stops do not stop while direct flights may stop several times, but the passengers do not change planes. Check with your travel agent or airlines if you have any doubt. Know how long your stopover will be, which city, location or airport the connection flights will be through, how much time in-between and if delayed what your options are.

16. **Forward thinking, anticipating, organizing and PLANNING all protect your travel interests, saves money and avoids unnecessary costs. A most helpful currency you have besides your travel funds and monetary resources is knowledge and information.** The more you know about the destinations and places you will be visiting, the more rewarding, and safe, enjoyable, memorable and fiscally successful your visit will be! A word to the wise: do not over- analyze and worry too much, constantly forgetting that this is about being a little spontaneous as well.

17. **In addition to the small bills amount you carry with you, transport most of your monetary funds in something like guaranteed travelers checks**. These are freely available through most local banks. Keep denominations to low figures is mostly advised. If however, you are worried about transaction fees on smaller amounts, get a couple of larger denominations to be on the safe side.

As a precautionary security measure, to save money and avoid difficulty, delay and inconvenience, remember to keep a list of the numbers of the checks somewhere separate from the checks themselves in case they are lost or stolen. Guard ATM and credit cards and do not carry all your money in one place!

18. **Verify medical conditions, travel and health advisories. Once you have picked your destination, it will serve you well to explore all health matters, including medical insurance and travel coverage you have and need.** Visit your medical practitioner/doctor prior to your trip to ask about immunizations prescriptions and more. Find out what basic and special medicines to take along. Ensure you know what to do in case of an emergency. Have the numbers and all insurance information handy.

19. **Optical tools like glasses and contact lenses, cleaning solutions, eyeglass repair kit etc, are all travel necessities if you wear them. Ensure they are on your pre-departure, out-the-door checklist.** Good advice to eyeglass-wearers: take an extra pair of glasses, as well as either a copy of the existing or a new prescription for your glasses, just in case you might need them.

20. **One of the most commonly made mistakes made by travelers is packing too much of everything.** Except for the inconvenience, there are also charges and fees for overages. You have to deal with having to ship personal belongings home, leaving some items at the airport, packing and unpacking bags, removing items and more! All these actions are responsive and costly options. Pack and travel light. Think minimalism when packing. Pick items that will suit and serve you well, multi-purpose, functional, mix and match well, are durable and easy-care. Essentials rather than outfit and accessory, fashion and color-coded planning dictating the bulging suitcase.

21. **A frequent-traveler favorite and luggage essential is the trusted small, lightweight travel alarm.** It will prove to come in handy repeatedly and is easily carried anywhere. They

are freely available and affordable from specialty travel stores as well as discount stores. Frequently travel alarms are sales items, so wait to make your purchase, if you can.

22. Checklists are helpful travel-enablers anywhere in the world at any phase of your trip. Some people write them out and a good tip to remember is that as you pack your bags, make a list of what you are taking. Expand the list if you buy anything while on your trip that will be going home with you. On the way home, having this checklist with you will help you avoid leaving or forgetting something along the way, in a bathroom or hotel drawer!

23. A laundry-saving tip suggests taking an ample supply of plastic bags to hold such things as soiled laundry, damp items and muddy shoes. These will protect and save your clothing and pocketbook in various ways. Small bags are excellent for storing toilet articles, stationery items, and medicine. You can also get specialized luggage storage space-saver, vacuum-type bags to maximize space in your suitcases and keep dirty and clean clothes separated and free from spills and leaks.

24. **Take a clean set of underwear and one change of clothes in your on-board or carry-on luggage.** It should ideally be packed with any valuables and items necessary to keep you happy, healthy and clean in case your checked luggage is misplaced, delayed or worse, stolen!

25. **Diaries, notebooks, and a couple of empty envelopes for note taking, budget-updates and receipts.** Many travelers keep diaries, scribbling not to forget experiences, sharing impressions, recording purchases, and or may we suggest, tracking your spending and budget.

Others might even use them to preparing suggestions for friends who might visit the same place in the future and or save their tax receipts in one place. It just provides travelers with a good way to record their travel tips and suggestions to share with others as well as having that first step towards your budget consolidation and next trip already started. This cuts down on the work you will have to do planning and budgeting for your next trip. You will avoid losing receipts for major purchases and have your proof of payment handy for any customs officer that asks you about it!

26. **Arrive early at the airport and allow enough time for security screenings and clearing customs.** Try getting to the airport at least two hours before your flight time on domestic flights and even earlier on international flights. A favorite or planned book to read or something fun to do will keep you occupied if you do end up having time on your hands.

You will be less stressed and rushed and enjoy your getting there part of your journey, starting the fun-part of your travel endeavor early. A positive travel attitude will focus on the fact that time passes quickly and with most boarding happening early these days due to security concerns it is definitely more crucial to be early rather than risking being refused at the boarding gate due to the new regulations. Plan for and depart in a timely, orderly fashion, in a more relaxed frame of mind and without incident. Be an empowered, action-oriented, pro-active perceptive traveler and you will be rewarded with a trip characterized by smooth sailing and good memories.

27. **To avoid having to pay more, incurring unplanned, additional costs and penalties for luggage overages pack S-M-A-R-T!** In preparing for your trip, after packing your luggage, lift it up, carry it around a block or two or down the stairs and see how it feels.

Remember, you will have to handle these eventually! This is a useful technique to re-evaluate and re-pack the amount you are taking with you. You will not be sorry. Also, leave some room for purchases while on your trip, as you would not like to have to buy additional pieces of luggage you do not really need, want, or incur costly shipping charges and or duties or other fees!

28. **If you are in for a long international or domestic flight, there are several suggestions for seeing it through. Enduring long hauls and not getting uncomfortable or bored** is the key here. A good night's sleep the night before, wearing comfortable, non-confining, wrinkle resistant clothes, and shoes that are fully broken in are all advisable.

Getting up regularly and walking around, making several trips to the washroom to wash your face and brush your teeth will keep you refreshed. Taking a casual stroll up and down the aisles of an airplane is a real lifesaver and keeps the circulation going. Avoid costly in-air, shopping catalogues, costly phone calls and frequent alcoholic drinks from the bar as all are prices at premium and will add up! Take along lots of water, snacks and reading materials. If you are traveling with kids, ensure toys, activities, and a cooled snack-pack for them too.

29. **Travel package deals always sound like such a bargain.** They mostly are priced better and lower, BUT before congratulating yourself though with a well-deserved pat on the back for a job well done and money saved, check the cancellation and refund policy. You need to know what happens when the inevitable occurs. Say you change your mind or a trip is canceled. Scrutinize the fine print and calculate what the financial impact would be. How much money will you likely lose or forfeit?

30. **Worried about the appearance of your luggage? Cannot afford new suitcases?** Does your travel-tools and luggage look worn, stained and on its last legs? Inspect your existing luggage, including zippers, wheels, handles and identification tags. Clean the exterior of leather luggage with a good liquid saddle soap and conditioner.

All canvas luggage can easily be cleaned using a small amount of detergent, 1 cup of water, and a scrub brush. Nylon and vinyl luggage takes mild detergent and a small amount of water to be wiped down. It is never a good idea to "soak" or immerse your suitcase in water. If this is still not enough and they are not salvageable, watch for retail sales, consider borrowing from a friend or relative or do the outlet, clearance and closeout circuits for bargains.

31. **Medical details should be on hand at all times.** Having any and all health related questions, information and emergency contacts and logistics, insurance and policy, immunization record (if applicable) and all other relevant documentation handy is key and can not be ignored. Preferably, also check with local providers if traveling alone, with children or special needs situations.

Research and inquire in advance, know or check upon arrival where the closest hospital, pharmacy and or clinic is, just for in case.

32. **Budgetary concerns and monitoring, fiscal restraint and disciplined spending when traveling will pay off.** When you are planning your trip and setting up your travel budget, taking into account things like ground transportation, tips and other incidentals, extras like laundry and mini-bar, room service, lodging and meals. Do the major obligations and essentials first. Then figure in expenses such as shopping, entertainment and foreign exchange fees for example. Not surprisingly at all, it is usually the impulse shopping or spur of the moment expenses

that let us over-spend and max-out our travel budget quickly or overspend.

33. **Concerned about appearances and wrinkled clothing? Save on laundry costs** with ingenuity and innovative solutions. Think practical and be creative. A frequent traveler suggests that if you travel with a small spray bottle, you can fill it with water, lightly spray the clothing, and let it hang for period. This usually helps the wrinkles fall out.

Another suggestion is hanging them in the bathroom while you take a hot shower or soak in the tub while the steam 'irons' out some of the creases. Hand-washing underwear, nylons etc. and hanging them up overnight is another sure saver and old frequent traveler favorite that has often been passed on by word of mouth!

34. **The importance of water or H20!!** Just like taking care of fueling the human engine with food, we also need lubrication. By that, we mean lots of fluid and specifically water. Staying hydrated, irrespective of the climate is just common sense. Invest in a good travel water bottle with a secure cap.

Always drink bottled water preferably – even when brushing your teeth or ordering your cocktails without ice or water if you are concerned about diseases etc. Drinking lots of water regularly will help prevent dehydration. You will also however have to plan for frequent pit stops for washrooms and remember in some countries you have to pay to use them! In air, on flight, just remember that alcohol can be extremely dehydrating and may increase jet lag on a long flight! So that's another good reason to drink lots of water.

35. **Insurance coverage is essential.** Not only travel, medical and cancellation insurance, but for valuables that will be accompanying you on the trip. These will be specified and additional coverage. It is still worth the small expense if weighed against loss or replacement cost without it should they get misplaced, forgotten or stolen. Insure your precious belongings and valuables before you leave home if you absolutely have to take them with you.

A great tip offered online at a travel website is to take along only what you are willing to lose. The rule of thumb and general agreement is still that it is much better to leave valuables at home.

36. **'Cash' only when you need to!** Only cash traveler's checks when you really need money. Take no risk of carrying too much cash with you for no real apparent reason. Avoid

being stuck with too much local currency from a foreign destination that you will lose money on if converting. Use all your small coins before changing notes. They make great tips! Minimize ATM and credit card transactions as they both carry transactional and administration fees – they are convenient but expensive.

37. **Guarding your identity, travel documentation and ensuring document accessibility is a travel priority.** Proof of identity and citizenship is your most prized travel possession. It is advised that you make at least two copies of your important documents, including your credit cards and passport. Keep one with you at all times and deposit the other in a safe place or leave it with a friend or family member or the hotel's safe. Have them handy and with you at all times. Never lose sight of your passport if you can help it and in case it is stolen, report it immediately as was stated earlier to avoid any difficulty, affecting your return home etc.

38. **Budget for passport and visa costs.** If you are planning a trip that requires a passport and or visa, check its expiration date. Be sure the passport is valid for the entire trip and that you have all the necessary entry-requirement documentation for your destination. There is lots of information

on the web on what you need where. Check with embassies and foreign offices in your own country and overseas to get the most accurate information. Verify this with a travel professional or travel agent prior to booking and departure. Remember to include this as a category on your budget worksheet.

39. **Plan and budget for the un-expected and incidentals.** Whether it is as simple as a practical collapsible type umbrella and poncho or a buffer-fund for in case there is a delay, extended stay or other factors where you will incur additional cost. Weather for example, is unpredictable and can ruin a travel experience if you let it. Again, the key to saving money, avoiding expense, caring for details and being a smart traveler will be organization, planning and fiscal preparedness and resourceful fiscal discipline.

40. **Maximize the packing space you have in your luggage.** While packing and making your checklist, put small items such as spare glasses, dress accessories, socks and other small items inside your shoes. Shoes are usually rigid and can protect items that might otherwise be broken. You will need every inch of your suitcases upon your return to avoid the battle of the 'bulging' suitcase that will not close until you go sit on it and struggle with the clasp until it finally closes!

41. Confirm the checkout time to avoid being billed for late checkout. Most hotels post a departure time when guests must vacate their rooms and advising the front desk immediately if there is a problem with this is prudent. Late checkouts are often permitted if approved by the hotel management in advance. Another way to ensure you get what you paid for is, when you are booking and or checking into a hotel, to request approval for late arrival/departure just as a precaution.

42. Save money on traveler's checks: Avoid paying a hefty or any service fee to purchase your travelers' checks. Some automobile clubs and banks offer them free to members and preferred customers. It is definitely worth your while and travel budget to check this out, before obtaining your checks.

43. Minor emergency tools and practical items in a handy spot in your luggage can prove to be a life and money-saver. A quick stop into the dollar store or local retailer before you leave home for a do-it-yourself kit that contains various small items like rubber bands, small tube of instant glue, paper clips, masking tape, Velcro, tissue-paper, sewing kit et al. could save you embarrassment, time and money! It is wise to toss something like this into your luggage. They take up limited space (will even fit in a shoe, as mentioned earlier), and can come in handy in solving minor emergencies.

44. **Sometimes a travel agent, or travel consultant, will charge a booking and administration fee to handle your trip and reservation**. This leads to the misconception that they are always expensive and overpriced, always costing more and higher priced. This simply is not the case.

Sometimes the opposite can be true. They are indeed also able to provide you with considerable information regarding special offers, limited time package deals and seat sales, as well as significantly reduced and special rates. They also offer advice and information about destination travel, travel advisories, entry requirements and travel documentation needs and costs. Upon request, they will also spend the time to find you the cheapest and discounted options in the marketplace. This is worthwhile considering if you want to maximize your travel dollar and have a dream destination or exotic vacation to remember.

45. **Another word to the wise when packing your luggage:** All things fluid and liquids in plastic bottles or containers should be placed in sealable plastic bags that will not leak. It is always wise to place the bottle into a well-sealed plastic bag as well. Wrapping a bottle in a towel or clothing will

not protect it or keep it from leaking and staining your clothes. The damage could be permanent and lead to unnecessary cost for laundry services and or replacement for clothes you really did not need or want.

46. **Avoid the duty-free lure and trap**. Typically, all shops in airports and train stations are expensive. It is a myth that you save money! Actually, compare the next time you try to buy liquor or souvenirs against reputable quality department stores. You might find to your surprise that the prices are higher!

47. **Staff and employees on location where you are staying are wonderful sources of information**. Do not hesitate to strike up a conversation or ask questions. This offers you with yet another avenue to secure valuable travel information and local tips and perspective. Asking for instructions, directions, advise and help will often be met with an eagerness to serve. Staff enjoy being of assistance to their guests and meaningfully contribute in any way, shape or form, that they can.

Remember your thoughtfulness for the room attendance, valet and bellhop (if applicable) with appropriate tips and a little note if you so choose to show your appreciation. If they are still there on any repeat visit, they will be sure to remember you!

48. **Be creative with meals and do not hesitate to improvise and eat like the locals**. For example, a picnic or a quick bite to eat on the beach or in a park is one of the best ways to keep your food costs down and save your travel dollar for the evenings and dinners out

49. **Be kind to your body, soul and mind!** Get enough sleep to stay alert and make good decisions. Weigh every purchase, outing and cost twice. Avoid spending impulses and impulsive shopping. If you just arrived at your destination, take a quick rest if you can and allow your body to adjust for time changes to come and recharge your batteries before venturing out.

50. **Take extreme care with keeping your personal documentation and possessions safe and under-eye.** Avoid endless headaches, red tape, delays and costly replacement and administration fees. Not to mention traveling to the nearest police station, long distance telephone calls home and to embassies and dignitaries to advise them of the situation is it is lost or stolen! Never leave money, valuables, or your passport unattended. **This is a strict rule, no exception -** Not even to go to the beach! Secure them at all times.

51. **Be brave and daring if you have or are traveling with someone with special needs.** It should not be a factor that makes you hesitant to travel at all. Most, if not all holiday service providers, airlines, hotels, campgrounds and attractions are usually very well equipped and prepared to accommodate unique requirements that could make your travel endeavor extremely memorable and pleasant.

Very seldom are there additional or hefty surcharges for special cabs and personalized service, assistance and specific needs and requirements you might have or face. Just ensure that all details have been taken care of in advance and that all providers have been notified at the time of booking, confirmation and re-confirmed just prior to arrival. Find allies and friends in the front desk staff and managers that they can give you the specialized customer attention you need and deserve at anytime you might require or request it.

52. **Local cuisine is a special treat. Ensure to budget for a couple of meals and outings where this is a priority!** If you budget for it specifically, you will not feel cheated into eating fast food or salads, for fear of over-spending or running out of travel dollars. Hotel restaurants are convenient, but more expensive typically.

53. **Personal freedom and safety also deserves a word to the travel wise.** If traveling in a group, you can venture out on your own. If you chose to do so, just always ensure that everyone knows where you are going, when you plan to return and do not miss-scheduled group-activities. Even if you are traveling by yourself, take steps to ensure your own personal safety and check that the areas and attractions you have chosen are safe and tourist-friendly, easily accessible and affordable and tell at least one other person where you are staying, where you are headed and what your plans are.

54. **A good way to rehearse for your trip** is to look at your own area or hometown as a destination as opposed to where you live and work. Ask yourself where you would go, what you would do and see. Also think about how you would get around ... all on a budget of course! This will not only not cost you money, but also get you into cost cutting and travel mode fairly quickly. There truly is nothing like lessons learnt and experience.

55. **Start the day off right.** One travel site advises that you might want to consider packing a "wake up kit". They typically can contain items like a travel mug, spoon, instant coffee or tea,

sweetener, dry creamer, and a plug-in immersion heater. It is a great way to start the day and you will save on the morning cupper or evening tea. Very important detail if every penny and travel dollar counts.

56. **Be resourceful and curious**. Know as much as you can about your destination and prepare as well as you can, even for the unexpected. Read any and all literature you can find on what you should know before departing, such as facts, warnings, advisories, entry requirements, crime statistics, demographics, local economy, attractions and special events for your dream destination.

Again, it is worth mentioning, that investing time, effort and yes, even money, if that is what it takes to get quality information that will save you money in the long run, will pay off! It is like a guaranteed investment in you and your travel dollar, pocketbook and budget.

57. **Medications and prescriptions**. If you have to travel with medicine, it is wise to carry it in the bottle the prescription came in to avoid any confusion during custom inspections. Even a note from your doctor to state what it is and what condition it is used for could be helpful. A copy of your prescription and or

even a refill prescription could be of value to you – especially on an extended trip.

58. **Multi-media and technology are travel essentials these days.** Recordings before, during and after can all be captured and enjoyed over and over. An added benefit is that they weight less and take up "no additional room".

It helps you assemble memories, so buying and budgeting for extra rechargeable batteries, charger- kits, adapter plugs, cables, carry-bags, memory cards and/or recordable media might very well be the best investment you make on and for your trip. For the return on investment is HUGE! Upon your return, it is always exciting to re-live key and precious, shared moments.

You could hear and view a tour guide, entertainers, or musicians enjoyed during your journey. Avoid buying and taking heavy travel guides with you (make copies of pages of interest). At your destination, there will always also be myriads of local sources at your disposal that offers a unique perspective, current pricing and information that might be outdated in even the most recent travel guides or magazines.

59. **When budgeting for any type of travel, package deal, or even your family vacation, find out about all costs associated with your trip.** Confirm with the agent, location or

provider you have chosen or listed on the flashy brochure or website you just visited. Read the fine print and avoid any surprises. Ask about alternatives, package deals, discounts, coupons and special offers – if you do not ask, you will never know. And also, no one is going to necessarily "advertise" a cheaper price or offer you the lowest, cheapest fare right away. There is always room for negotiation and or innovative ways to cut costs and still have a memorable trip to an exotic destination.

60. **Another money strategy includes having a personal check or two with you.** They are not accepted any and everywhere, BUT where they are, they are cheaper than credit card transactions.

61. **Giving tips are considered common courtesy and customary most places in the world.** BUT as an expenditure category, it can add up quickly and substantially! If ever in doubt whether it is appropriate to give a tip, ASK! Ensure you set aside enough of an incidental budget to cover these and other daily expenditures covering the duration of your trip.

62. **A minimum investment for maximum payback**! Something as simple as clearly marking and tagging your luggage, can be the difference between no additional money

spent and or possessions lost or misplaced, for lost 'indefinitely' or mishandled luggage seemingly nowhere to be found.

This makes it more traceable and easy to spot. Clearly, it is a worthwhile investment to buy a sharpie or permanent marker and some quality luggage tags. If your budget does not allow for this, consider using the airline or provider tags at your departure location. Never travel with an unmarked bag that does not carry your name and information on it. This ensures traceability and do not even hesitate to put some identifying characteristic element on it, like a colorful ribbon, sticker or other identifier that will make it stand out.

63. **Carry-on luggage is a stopgap solution for inevitabilities and a safe haven for valuables**. See it as your all-in-one solution to anything that can be thrown at you. Remember not to pack any dangerous or forbidden items in your on-flight baggage. It is a good idea to take a change of clothes in your on-flight bag for every person in your travel party.

64. As mentioned earlier **rechargeable batteries and a charger kit are not bad ideas** to avoid bulk and additional cost of replacing it or worse not being able to take the footage or pictures you want, because the power has run low or out. These

priceless memories and their enablers need to be budgeted for as well by the money-wise traveler, taking care of even the littlest of details to ensure a memorable trip.

65. **When we travel, we tend not to think too much about nutrition and good diet**. The last thing you want to do is spend more money upon your return on a personal trainer or weight management program to battle the holiday bulge and extra vacation pounds you have gained.

Ensure a healthy, balanced eating style, habit and choices, with the occasional indulgence and treat as opposed to throwing all caution into the wind and making it all about the food. There are so many other activities to partake in, do not let boredom drive you to the only thing most people end up doing on vacation – eating and then way too much usually.

66. **Arrange for house sitters and emergency contact numbers and information at home, while you are away.** To save on costs for home security, burst pipes, fire and other emergencies or burglaries, ask a neighbor or close trusted friend to keep a watchful eye on your behalf and drop in from time to time to water plants, shovel driveways and collect mail, junk mail and newspapers. Reward them with a special and

thoughtful memento or dinner invite or both (depending on your budget) upon your return. Leave your itinerary with your friends, relatives, neighbors, or co- workers. They may need to contact you. Smart travelers start at home!

67. **Arm yourself with personal information.** Having all your bank contact telephone numbers written down on a piece of paper, packed in your luggage and somewhere else on your person or in the hotel safe in an envelope with your other valuables you want under lock and key is the best way to protect your financial interest. Finding out in advance who to call in case your checks or credit cards are lost or stolen is very important and will save you time and money and minimize the impact of any theft and or aftermath of lost, misplaced or stolen cards, wallets and travelers checks.

68. **Keeping valuables safe and have peace of mind at the same time.** Hotel safes or security boxes or even in-room/wall-mounted, combination locks and safes are options for storing your possessions that your treasure and value.

69. **Always layer and/or take a sweater or multi-purpose jacket with you, wherever you go.** It can get cool

pretty fast and a tourist location is not the place to have to buy this item. They will be priced a little higher obviously and you would probably spend too much without a second thought just because you need one! Not a good decision for your travel budget necessarily – especially if it is an unbudgeted item. That is where the checklist comes in handy when packing your suitcase in the first place. Planes can also be very cool spaces, so ask for a blanket and pillow when you sit down in your seat.

70. A good piece of advice around dealing with vacation shopping, declarations, receipts and customs officials: Having it all in one-place speeds up the process. If shopping is part of your travel endeavor and enjoyment on your trip, pack a flat fabric bag in the bottom of your suitcase.

When returning from your trip place all the purchased items in this bag. Everything is accessible and saves you time and money! If not, at the very least, you have made one official's life a little easier today and your reward will be a smile, stamp and a nod!

71. **Personal identification tags or information for all travelers, especially young kids**! It does not hurt to keep a list of credit card numbers, telephone numbers, and driver license

information in a convenient location such as a purse or wallet. You never know when you might need it to either prove your identity, for a major purchase or car rental, in emergencies and numerous other reasons. A resourceful traveler is always prepared for anything!

72. **Dental care kits**. Most people think of a toothbrush and toothpaste, maybe even floss and mouthwash. But did you ever stop to think of taking an 'emergency dental kit" when you travel?

Some items in this customized, personalized dental kit could include: aspirin or aspirin substitute, small container of hydrogen peroxide and water, dental floss, a dental mirror, and gauze. If you do have a medical or dental emergency, get and ask for references and discuss costs and coverage in full with your chosen or available provider.

73. **A unique suggestion for the budget**-wise traveler is to keep a spending log as you go about your shopping endeavors. List all of your purchases. Include what you paid in foreign currency and the equivalent in U.S. dollars. No time wasted calculating customs duties and fees. The added bonus is everything is at your fingertips when the time comes to do the

next travel budget! You will be one-step ahead this time round and even better prepared.

74. Pre-paid phone cards are a great idea for gifts for travelers. They are a good alternative to long distance from your hotel-room, cabin or any-place else on location where you find yourself vacationing. Today people also choose to use cell phones and text-messages to stay in touch and remain connected. Both are good options to save money while traveling.

75. A budget-travel provider provides us with this quote: "Remember this advice for sightseers: Never stand when you can sit, never sit when you can lie down, and never pass up a chance to use the bathroom" Translated into our model, savor every opportunity, embrace every chance provided that does not cost you anything, embrace hospitality, gifts and extended generosity. A nickel and a dime here and there saves dollars in the end!

76. Secure and make change as soon as you can after arriving at your destination. This will avoid having to revert to your smaller denomination bills and tipping with a heavy hand

and even heavier heart! This is a sure way not to deplete your incidental travel budget category.

77. Another nutritional tip to save some money: Do not skip meals in order to save money! It is mostly counter-productive as most possibly, you would need medication for headaches as your blood-sugar drops and overall it is not worthwhile jeopardizing the rest of your trip in this fashion.

It is in fact not economizing and SMART traveling at all skipping meals. Travel activity and sightseeing takes energy. Fuel your human engine. Fresh fruit and local produce offer good alternatives to fast food or hefty restaurant bills.

78. **Special dietary requirements need special budgeting and attention to detail.** Specifying this up-front is crucial to avoid any surcharges and or additional cost for special meals. For most travel providers it is no problem. Shopping at a local grocer, market or deli are all ways to stretch that "meal" ticket and travel dollar just a little further. If you are in a self-contained unit with its own kitchen and fridge, you can cut your costs even further by buying some essentials and snacks, small

meals in-room will cut down meal and entertainment expenses tremendously.

79. **Be SMART and check all details of tourist locations and attractions, pricing and more before departing to the location or event.** Always check the admission and operating hours. It is very disappointing to find things closed when you expect them to be open. Remember to check on special holidays as well. Do not spend or waste the money on the ground-transportation to get your all the way there and back – only to be deeply disappointed!

80. **Mostly people say time is money!** Generally, true, indulge a bit in this category and give yourself some free or spare time for visiting a fascinating place, a special shop, or a hidden off-the- beaten path so to speak item, place or activity you really do not want to or cannot miss! Do not over-extend or over-schedule yourself. There are only 24 hours in a day after all!

81. **Multi-tools and pocketknives have always been useful and advisable**. In a climate of the threat of terrorism however, it is definitely preferable not to carry it in your

backpack or cabin- luggage. It needs to be packed in your checked luggage if you choose to take them at all. Alternatively, if you are flying and still think you might have a need for one – ask the concierge where you can buy one cheaply for camping, trekking, or other adventure travel.

82. Travel-custom accessories like a collapsible cup are worth a lot. For those times and every moment when you need some water from a fountain, faucet or hose to re-hydrate! This is an inexpensive item to invest in that will not break the budget one bit and save you money in the process and is light to pack. This is a must-have for any would-be traveler – especially those traveling with young kids.

83. Free-style cruising has become a popular choice for those who prefer a truly leisure-style vacation. It is highly open and leaves tourists with the final option and decision on what and when they want to participate in. This is your trip, so just remember that any of the offshore excursions normally have to be paid for separately. In some cases, any drinks and alcohol is additional too. Family cruises and all-inclusive options also offer good alternatives for most budgets.

84. **Back-up plans for 'energy-sources' for your technology devices.** It was suggested earlier that you take rechargeable batteries and a charge kit with you. It could also be prudent perhaps, to carry a spare set of batteries for your camera, radio, camcorder and other multi-media devices. Batteries are not always available overseas and often cost considerably more.

85. **Do not overburden yourself with an overwhelming schedule that will leave you feeling like you need the vacation when you arrive back home from your trip.** Maximizing and optimizing your budget and trip does not mean doing everything thinkable, imaginable and under the sun, that you can afford and fit in! You are doing a disservice to the purpose, goal and process that is savvy traveling!

A travel regular advises online that you should not feel that you have to do everything to get your money's worth. There is not a thing wrong with relaxing and taking a breather along the way.

86. **Carrying identification and hotel or resort location information and telephone number on your person is**

advisable. The easiest way is to simply ask the front-desk attendant for a business card when you check in. This again will save you time and money. It comes in extremely handy should you ever get lost and need to find your way or for taxi drivers. Might even save a buck or two!

87. **Budget categories often overlook include gifts for others.** If you are purchasing souvenirs and mementos for friends, leave some money in a discretionary or personal allowance category. If running low on capital a personalized post-card mailed from the location is always seen as thoughtful and valued because others feel flattered that you took the time to think about them and buy, write and sent it.

Does your budget allow gifts? Then do make a list prior to your departure with all you want to purchase gifts for and the amount you want to or can spend. Check the names off as you make your purchases. Avoid utilizing your credit card as we tend to over-spend and over-extend ourselves, just by default almost of not having to pay for it then and there with ready cash.

88. There are lots of frequently asked questions online at travel provider websites that can give good tips and answers to

some of the situations, ,questions and issues that you might have that we have not specifically addressed here.

89. **Utilize and optimize local knowledge**, customs and hospitality. Learn, accept and appreciate the customs of the country you are visiting. Go with the flow and enjoy the culture, music, food and kindness of the area and its people! Sometimes you will be surprised that it does not even cost you a cent to have a good time and share with others.

90. **Instant Polaroid cameras and disposables are getting smaller and smaller**. Invest in a couple for those off-the-beaten track moments or people who want a snapshot of themselves. Share moments and memories inexpensively while making good friends along the way! Nothing can be better (and cheaper) than that.

91. **Do not sweat the small stuff**. If you cannot afford tipping near the end of your trip due to a drained budget, do not worry about tipping! A heartfelt thank you or honest explanation, smile and kindness, even a hand with the luggage is sometimes enough for people to know you care and appreciate their effort, gesture and service.

92. An inexpensive, fold-up raincoat or poncho can be a life and money-saver. Always have either that or the collapsible umbrella mentioned earlier with you. Being prepared for the occasional downpour is better than being soaked and getting sick in the process.

93. A staple essential is tissue and toilet paper in your shoulder bag. Some suggest toilet seat covers as well. Hygiene will go long way to protect you from disease and illness. Something you definitely do not need while on vacation is getting sick or infected! Hand sanitizer and wipes are other small travel essential you can consider for your pockets or travel bag when you are out and about your dream destination, taking in the sights.

94. Be SMART and informed about public holidays, special events, concerts and attractions in the countries and areas you plan to be visiting. By doing your homework early and coming up with budgetary categories and discretionary funds for entertainment and special events helps you with priorities, plan itineraries, save and execute a memorable and unforgettable trip.

95. **Seating arrangements on the plane can be done in advance or at time of booking even.** Ensure you get what is comfortable for you, verify upon check-in, and boarding that you have what you need, requested and paid for. Who knows, you might just score and upgrade if seats are available.

This is also important for parents traveling with infants, special needs and pregnant passengers and travelers alike. Save money, avoid additional costs, ensure detail and be SMART when you book your flights, early or late, with specific seating requirements or without stating preference. It is all up to you to personalize, customize, plan and budget for your perfect vacation!

96. **Utilize local resources and access their expertise knowledge** in order to cut down on costs. Get information and coupons for special attractions, family passes and two-for-one offers, free coupon booklets or special discounted offers and tickets you might not be able to find anywhere else. They also send material and guides in advance that can help you plan, budget, compare and decide when, where, how and why, soon, sooner, soonest!

97. **Another money-saver is a travel accessory often overlooked: a lightweight plastic flask** can also be filled with water, fruit juice, or whatever you prefer is a good budgeting trick. Carry it in your shoulder bag and again resist the urge to splurge! Even if it is just on a coffee, bottled beverage or alcoholic beverage to quench your thirst!

98. **Budget for inexpensive but thoughtful regional gifts for friends at home or newly made friends abroad alike.** Packaged flower seeds are a good option

99. **Always verify your luggage allowances and flight details**. Valued advice from another frequent traveler serves us well here to stretch our dollar: 'Without exception, always check in advance on the amount of luggage you may take. Planes, trains and motor coaches, all have regulations regarding amount and size of luggage. It is considered courtesy to stick to their requirements and can save you a lot of embarrassment, added expense, aggravation, and trouble.'

100. **Another final, last minute check**: as mentioned earlier, it is advisable to check every detail and aspect of your luggage. This will include the handles, wheels and zippers on

every suitcase and bag before leaving on your trip. Be sure and budget for the worst-case scenario that you have to replace your luggage and suitcase. If it ends up not being necessary, you have a little bit of extra cash to treat yourself and some discretionary budget spending!

101. **People often say the only thing you really need to travel is money and a sense of humor**. We hope that this guide provided you useful insights on both. There is a lot of truth on both sides of this spectrum.

A final word

Remember that having a plan, budget, positive outlook, patience and understanding, flexibility, and a little human kindness goes a long way as you globetrot your way through this wonderful world.

We trust that these 101 tips and general discussion and suggestions serve you well. We wish you all the best on your travel endeavors as you work your way down your checklist of dream destinations. Discover and visit corners of the earth you never thought possible before, on more than just a wing and a prayer!

Bon Voyage!!

Addendum

A typical packing checklist

- 2 pairs of pants
- 3-4 shirts
- A dark-colored sweater that is best to wear en route
- Clothes for a dressy occasion, for comfort while traveling and suitable to the climate
- One sport-jacket for men (some restaurants require them)
- Swimsuit
- Cover-up for beach or pool
- Raincoat and galoshes
- Hat, beret or sun hat
- 3-5 pairs of underwear
- 5 pairs of socks – cotton or wool
- Sleepwear
- 1 pair of sturdy well-broken in boots or sandals

- If for winter travel include down jacket, waterproofed boots, gloves and hat and long underwear

Other suitable items for purse of carry-on luggage:

Passport   Pens and pencils

Tickets   Camera, film, batteries

Itinerary   Multi-media accessories

Traveler's checks   Zip-lock or plastic bags (seal)

International certificate of vaccination   Dictionary

or phrasebook

Maps   Laundry items - detergent

Money belt of pouch   Clothes-brush

Extra glasses, contact lenses and prescriptions

Inflatable hanger or two

Combination lock   Rubber sink stopper

Address , notebook or journal and small pad of paper

First aid kit - bandages

Daypack   Moleskin for blisters

Pocket flashlight for each traveler   Analgesic

Net shopping bag   Antiseptic towelettes

Travel alarm clock   Insect repellent

Sunglasses   Anti-malaria pills

Thermometer in hard case   Nail clipper & Tweezers

Toiletries	Optional
Toothbrush and paste, extra dental floss	Ear plugs and eye shade
Soap and soap dish	Binoculars in hard case
Shampoo	Roll of transparent tape
Moisturizer	Adapter
Lip balm	Transistor radio,
CD or walkman,	MP3player
Small towel and washcloth	Musical instrument (if appropriate)
Hairbrush or comb	
Razor, blades and shaving cream	

Checklist when traveling with children: (infants or toddlers)

Car seat with cloth liner	Small packets of tissues
Disposable diapers	Nightlight
Wet-ones	Flashlight
Change pad	Extra juice
Garbage bags	Childs cup with drinking spout
Diaper rash ointment	Collapsible cup
Fork and spoon	Drinking straws

Familiar foods (cereal, crackers and noodles)   Finger foods (cubes of cheese, vegetable sticks)

Vitamins of fluoride drops	Bibs
Small toys	pencils and pads of paper
Favorite animal or doll	Pacifier
Compass	Transparent tape
Insect repellent	Baby shampoo and soap
Favorite books	

A wise traveler once said: "Take half the clothes and twice the money!"

Try to resist the urge to pack everything "just in case" and all but the kitchen sink.

The secrets to selecting and packing well: pack light, adaptable and comfortable clothing, do not buy an all new wardrobe prior to traveling, comfortable shoes, cotton or wool socks as you will be doing a lot of walking, underwear, avoid expensive clothes that you are sorry for, washability, durability and color, mix-and-match, accessorize to bring variety, layer and adjust to the climate.

Other money considerations when traveling:

Foreign exchange - Changing money

Look for the best rate and be aware of banking hours

Familiarize yourself with how the process and exchange rate actually works Clarify any fees associated with the transaction

Know the local currency and be able to tell them apart

Bring a small pocket calculator to assist you with quick conversions Save all your receipts

Combine your monetary instruments and travel funds

Cash, credit cards and traveler's checks, preferably carried on-person, in a money-belt

ATM systems

Available, accessible, convenient and expensive Transaction fees for cash withdrawals

Set Dollar limit daily on what you can withdraw

Credit card withdrawals will require a PIN code – get this by calling the toll-free # or your local bank prior to your departure

Bring Visa and Master card – not all machines accept all cards

You will receive local currency, not dollars. You will be billed accordingly to the exchange rate on the day the charge clears at home, not the rate in effect on the day of the transaction

Traveler's checks

Safest way to have your travel funds with you Receive a better exchange rate than cash typically Get them early and lock in your rate Denominations (small and large preferred)

Keep a record: city and date or purchase, amount and numbers

Update your record daily, keep better track of your spending, budget, and cash still in-hand You will need a passport to cash your traveler's checks

Immediately report any stolen or lost checks

Credit cards

Convenient and safe to use

Postpones immediate payment for transportation, lodgings, purchases and so on Can assist you to get access to cash

Beware of overspending Watch the exchange rates Credit card acceptance varies

Different cards have different perks Protect your credit cards

Check and keep all your charge slips – these will be used for budgeting and expense consolidation

Red Tape and documents you should take on a trip abroad:

Travel documentation: tickets, passport and visas Copy of naturalization certificate

Birth certificate

Driver's license and international driver's permit Travel insurance claims form

Extra passport photos – at least half a dozen

Any membership cards, like AAA membership, retired, veteran or student cards

Basic medical information, blood type, allergies, doctor's address, prescription refill and extra prescription medications you may require Immunization cards

"IF YOU GO ONLY ONCE AROUND THE ROOM, YOU ARE WISER THAN HE WHO STANDS STILL"

Estonian Proverb

There are numerous popular and well-read, published, copyrighted materials and even out of print sources and books available on travel in general. Some are general and others deal specifically with budgeting for business, leisure or vacation travel. General references are made to some of the sources used in this summary. This is complemented by an increasing amount of quality online publications, sources and travel sites, specifically named and credited here for their contributions to the body of knowledge on travel. Through state-of-the-art, budget travel-sites and dollar-saver clubs, they openly share travel insights and offer money-saving options for travelers to explore in the public domain. This proud tradition will continue.

Printed by Libri Plureos GmbH in Hamburg,
Germany